Finding Out About

VICTORIAN ENGINEERING

Alan Evans

B.T. Batsford Limited, *London*

Contents □□□□□□

ACKNOWLEDGMENTS

The Author and Publishers would like to thank the following for their permission to reproduce illustrations: the editor of The Engineer for pages 5, 27, 29, 31, 34 and 39; Michael Rawcliffe for pages 14, 16, 28 and 30. The map on page 46 was drawn by R.F. Brien. The photographs on pages 3, 5 and 7 are from the Author's collection.

Frontispiece

One of the central sections of the Forth Bridge under construction.

Cover illustrations

The colour illustration is a hand-coloured engraving of the Clifton Suspension Bridge; the black and white engraving shows the Great Eastern *paying out the Atlantic cable; the advertisement is from Harvey & Co.'s* Hayle Foundry Catalogue, *1884.*

© Alan Evans 1987
First published 1987

Typeset by Tek-Art Ltd, Kent
and printed in Great Britain by
R.J. Acford
Chichester, Sussex
for the publishers
B.T. Batsford Limited,
4 Fitzhardinge Street
London W1H 0AH

ISBN 0 7134 5154 8

Introduction ▢▢▢

Engineering is to do with the designing, building and maintaining of machines, the construction of roads and bridges, of electrical equipment, and so on. An engineer is someone who does this work. This book is about engineers and engineering during the reign of Queen Victoria, 1837-1901. A lot of the great engineering works of that period still exist and many of the engineering advances made then have helped to lay the foundations of the Britain we know today.

In many ways the Victorian period, and especially the years up to about 1860, was the great age of engineering in Britain. It was then that famous engineers like Robert Stephenson, I.K. Brunel, Henry Bessemer and Joseph Locke carried out their work. After 1860, however, engineering began to change; it began to get more specialized. In the 1830s when Brunel built the Great Western Railway, he not only laid out the track and built the tunnels and bridges, he also designed virtually every piece of equipment on the line. Fifty years later the engineer would confine himself to the surveying of the line, leaving the design of bridges and tunnels to another engineer or to a contractor. Stations would be designed by an architect, signalling would be installed by a specialist firm, and the track and rolling stock

The Brunel Atmospheric Railway engine house at Starcross near Exeter in Devon.

would be provided by the railway company. This specialization is called "division of labour". It meant that engineering became a team effort and that no one person's name could be linked to the finished product. An educated man in 1860 would have been able to tell you that Paxton designed the Crystal Palace and Brunel the "Great Eastern". Few people today could say who was responsible for the Forth Road Bridge or a particular section of the M25 motorway.

The engineer as we know him today dates back to the later eighteenth century, to the time of the Industrial Revolution. Engineers came from three main sources. First from the blacksmiths, wheelwrights and carpenters. From these men, skilled in the use of wood and metal, came the millwright, the man who could design machines. Secondly, for several hundred years there had been men expert in the making of navigational instruments, weapons, clocks and similar items. They had the precision skills that some types of Victorian engineers would need. Lastly, for thousands of years soldiers had known how to build tunnels, roads and fortifications. These abilities would be used by the great civil engineers of the nineteenth century. Thus, when Britain began to industrialize late in the eighteenth and early nineteenth century, she had men with the necessary skills to build machines and improve communications. By 1860 Britain was "the workshop of the world" and her engineers, who played such a vital part in that development, were greatly admired, both at home and abroad.

The words "engineer" and "engineering" are difficult to use. This is because "engineer" can mean at least two different things, and because there are so many different kinds of engineering. An "engineer" can be someone who designs and supervises a project – and it is with this sort of engineer that this book is mainly concerned – but an engineer can also be the skilled craftsman who makes a machine, working from plans drawn up by someone else. In America an "engineer" is also the man who drives a train.

Civil engineering and mechanical engineering are the two main types of engineering and are the ones with which this book deals. At the start of the nineteenth century it was possible for one man to be both a civil and a mechanical engineer: George Stephenson and his son laid out railway lines and designed locomotives. However, as engineering developed so engineers became more specialized. The civil engineer stuck to his roads and railway lines and the mechanical engineer to the design of machines and tools. By 1901 specialization had gone much further. By then there were agricultural, electrical, gas, hydraulic, telegraph and telephone, sanitary, mining and marine engineers. Today the list of specializations is much larger and includes production, structural, chemical, aeronautical, biochemical, biomedical, nuclear and offshore engineers.

In 1873 the author of a history of England could write:

> **It is to British engineers that the world owes railways . . . . To them it owes the fleets of iron ships . . . . To them it owes the ocean telegraph . . .**

In 1985 the Engineering Council in an advertisement painted a very different picture:

(i) **After the war [1939-1945] Great Britain was the third largest steel producer; now we are the tenth.**

(ii) **In 1900 Great Britain made 60% of the world's shipping; today we make 3%.**

(iii) **Before the war almost every car on our roads was British; now well over half are foreign.**

(iv) **Great Britain pioneered the world's machine tool industry; now our share is 3.1%.**

(v) **We once made all the textile machinery in the world; we now make 8%.**

I hope this book will not only help you to find out about Victorian engineering but will also make you think about how and why British engineering supremacy has declined in this century.

Useful Sources

There are many ways you can find out about Victorian engineering. This book tells you about some of them and you will discover more when you carry out your own research.

1. PEOPLE TO ASK

Your nearest large library will have all sorts of useful information. The librarians will be able to give you advice on what to read, especially if you are clear about the sort of information you are looking for. Sections 3a and 4 contain examples of sources which may be found in larger libraries. You may also find in the library details of local history societies and clubs. Perhaps they have a junior section which you can join.

2. THE LOCAL AREA

The best way of finding out about Victorian engineering is to visit actual sites. For instance, there are over 60,000 railway bridges in Britain, most of them built over 100 years ago. Of course, not all of them are very interesting but wherever you live there is likely to be an impressive Victorian bridge or railway viaduct nearby. Take photographs and try to calculate measurements, but do not trespass on the railway! Take advantage of family outings, holidays and school trips to build up an album of photographs. Reference books from your library will give you dates of construction and precise measurements.

3. VISUAL MATERIAL

a) *Photographs* Your local history library might have a collection of nineteenth-century photographs of your area. Some of these might well show you what local bridges etc. looked like 100 years ago.

b) *Paintings* If you live in a large town you might find that your local municipal art gallery has nineteenth-century paintings and prints of local engineers and their work.

c) *Machinery* Many museums have models of machines and some have real machines still in working order. Postcards of these machines are often available and are useful for projects. See Places to Visit at the back of this book for a list of useful museums.

The Royal Albert Bridge crossing the Tamar.

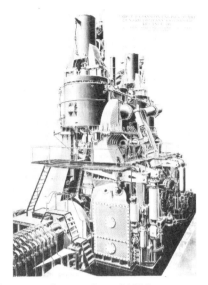

A triple expansion engine of 1893.

d) *Maps and plans* Ordnance Survey maps are useful for pinpointing railways, bridges, etc. Books on engineering and engineers often contain plans of engineering works.

4. WRITTEN SOURCES

a) *Memoirs and biographies* Many of the leading Victorian engineers wrote accounts of their lives and Samuel Smiles wrote vividly about many of them in his books. Some of these books have been reprinted and your local public library will be able to get them for you. In the reference section of larger libraries you will find the multi-volume *Dictionary of National Biography* (1893) which is a very useful source of information about nineteenth-century engineers.

b) *Contemporary descriptions of railways and other engineering projects* Some of these are also being reprinted. Two recent examples are *The Illustrated Guide to the Great Western Railway* (1852), which is on sale in bookshops, and *The Railway Companion, Describing an Excursion along the Liverpool Line* (1833), which is available at the North Western Museum of Science and Technology. You may find that in your area local history societies or the museum service have reprinted similar material.

c) *Local histories, trade directories, guide books and company catalogues* You will find that local history libraries usually contain materials like these on your own area. They often give useful descriptions in words and pictures of all sorts of engineering works.

d) *Old newspapers* The reference or local history section of your main library will probably contain copies of nineteenth-century national and local newspapers (sometimes these are on micro-film). From these you can get descriptions of bridges, viaducts and the like at the time when they were officially opened. They sometimes also contain advertisements for local engineering firms.

c) *Modern newspapers* These can be a surprisingly useful source of information. In the year 1984-5 there have been articles in papers like *The Times*, the *Daily Telegraph* and the *Guardian* on a fire in a nineteenth-century railway tunnel, collapsing Victorian sewers, the celebration of the one hundred and fiftieth anniversary of the Great Western Railway and the one hundred and twenty-fifth anniversary of the Royal Albert Bridge. Your school and local library will probably have copies of these papers.

5. TELEVISION AND RADIO

These are sources of information which you should not neglect. For instance, there have been television programmes linked to the one hundred and fiftieth anniversary of the Great Western Railway and one recent children's programme looked at the building of the Crystal Palace in 1851. Radio also celebrates the anniversaries of important events. Local television and radio programmes can also sometimes provide interesting news. In August 1985, for example, the re-opening of the nineteenth-century Summit Tunnel under the Pennines was featured in local news programmes.

Today professional engineers have a university or polytechnic degree in engineering or qualifications of a similar standard, but few engineers at work in the 1830s and 1840s had what we would call a proper training.

THE EDUCATION OF GEORGE STEPHENSON

In later life Stephenson enjoyed telling about the difficulties he had had to face in his youth:

> . . . if he had enjoyed the opportunity which most young men now have [i.e. in the 1840s], of learning from books what previous experimenters had accomplished, he would have been spared much labour and mortification. Not being acquainted with what other mechanics had done, he groped his way in pursuit of some idea originated by his own independent thinking and observation [and then] found that his supposed invention had long been known and recorded in scientific books . . . . Yet his very struggle to overcome the difficulties which lay in his way, was of itself an education of the best sort. (S. Smiles, *The Lives of the Engineers*, Vol. III, 1862).

If you do some research on George Stephenson you will soon find out why he had no scientific books when he was a young man. Why do you think that Smiles felt that this trial and error process was a good education? Do you agree?

THE YOUNG JAMES NASMYTH

Nasmyth was to be one of the great Victorian mechanical engineers. In his account of his life, published in 1883, Nasmyth described how he persuaded the famous Henry Maudsley to train him.

> It was the summit of my ambition to get work in that establishment [i.e. Maudsley's workshop] . . . . I determined to try what I could do towards attaining my object by submitting to Mr. Maudsley actual specimens of my capability as a young workman and draughtsman . . . he desired me to bring my models [of steam engines] for him to look at . . .

This picture is taken from a working man's magazine of 1858. Notice the locomotive and the navvies. What message is the magazine trying to put across?

Engineers □□□□□□□

EDUCATION IN THE WORKSHOP

In a speech to a meeting of mechanical engineers in Newcastle in 1858 Robert Stephenson defended a practical education for engineers as opposed to one gained from books.

> ... the more my experience has advanced, the more convinced I have become that it is a necessity to educate an engineer in the workshop. That is, emphatically, the education which will render the engineer most intelligent, most useful, and the fullest of resources in times of difficulty.

What do you think is the best way to train an engineer – at university from books and lectures, or by practical experience, or by a mixture of the two?

The Institute of Mechanical Engineers, not far from the Houses of Parliament in London. The building was opened in 1899. What does the building tell you about the importance of engineers in Victorian Britain?

THE TAUNTON COMMISSION

In 1864 Mathew Arnold submitted a report on the training of engineers to the Taunton Commission, which was investigating the educational system in Great Britain.

> Our engineers have no real scientific instruction, and we let them learn their business at our expense by rule of thumb, but it is a ruinous system of blunder and plunder. A man without the requisite scientific knowledge undertakes to build a difficult bridge; he builds three which tumble down, and so learns to build a fourth which stands, but somebody pays for the three failures. In France or Switzerland he would not have been suffered to build his first bridge until he had satisfied competent persons that he knew how to build it.

> then and there he appointed me to be his own private workman, to assist him in his little paradise of a workshop, furnished with the models of improved machinery and engineering tools of which he has been the great originator.

See if you can find out more about Nasmyth and Maudsley in an encyclopaedia. Then see if your local library has any of the books by Smiles and Rolt listed on p. 47. What does a draughtsman do today?

By the end of the nineteenth century prospective engineers learned the theory of engineering at mechanics' institutes, technical colleges and universities. Ask your careers teacher for information on the entry requirements and training programmes for the various levels of engineer today.

The Engineer's Life

The life of successful engineers like R. Stephenson, I.K. Brunel and J. Locke during the first half of Queen Victoria's reign was a very busy one. Although such men were well paid (Joseph Locke, for example, was able to buy a country estate and enter Parliament), all three were to die in their mid-fifties, worn out by over work.

JOSEPH LOCKE

The Times in its obituary on Locke on 20 September 1860 described some of his achievements. He first completed the Grand Junction line from Manchester to Birmingham (1835-7) and then:

> The Lancaster and Preston line was . . . commenced in 1837, and was opened in 1840, in which latter year the Sheffield and Manchester line was also undertaken. Some time previous to the completion of the Grand Junction line a railway from London to Southampton had been also commenced . . . the whole main line was completed on the 11th of May, 1840 . . .
>
> From Southampton it was natural that he should turn to France, where numerous projects were subsequently set on foot by him as engineer – as, for example, the Paris and Rouen and Rouen and Havre lines . . . a line from Paris to Lyons; and the Caen and Cherbourg line which was opened in 1856 . . . [together with his partner from 1840, Locke also] constructed the Lancaster and Carlisle, the East Lancashire, the Caledonian, the Scottish Central, the Scottish Midland, and the Aberdeen Railways, and the Greenock Railway and Docks.

Notice that Locke worked on several lines at once and that (like other British engineers at this time) he also worked abroad. Why do you think Locke took on a partner and why was it "natural" that he should have turned to France?

Daniel Gooch in 1845.

"NO ORDINARY MAN"

In 1858, in an article entitled "The Difficulties of Railway Engineering", published in *Quarterly Review*, the anonymous author pointed out:

> The Railway engineer . . . must be no ordinary man. First of all he must act as a surveyor in laying out a practical road [line], exercising his judgement as a geologist in determining the lie of the strata and the materials to be penetrated, testing them by careful borings with a view to the preliminary

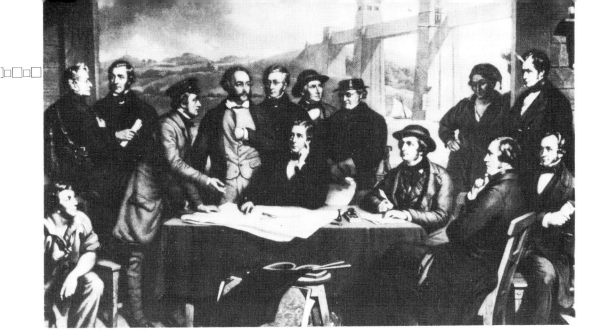

WAGES

Daniel Gooch, the locomotive superintendent on the G.W.R., recorded in his *Memoirs and Diary*, published in 1892:

> On 15th January [1846] the directors of the Great Western increased my salary by £300 a year. When I first joined the Great Western [1837] my salary was fixed at £300 but when the line opened it was increased to £550 and in January 1841 to £700; the increase now made it £1,000. It was raised on the 1st January

estimates, and the letting of the works. After satisfying Committees [of Parliament] in the face of cross-questionings by learned counsel, he must then enter upon the most anxious part of his labours – the actual construction of the railway.

Before a railway could be built Parliament had to give its approval. Those who opposed the proposed line would hire lawyers to question the engineer in charge. You will find details of this procedure in biographies of the great engineers.

A conference of engineers in 1849 in a hut on the edge of the Menai Straits. (The painting is by John Lucas.) Robert Stephenson is at the centre of the table with Locke and Brunel sitting to his left. Can you see the two navvies and the Britannia Bridge in the background?

> 1851 to £1,500, at which it stood until I left the service [1864].

An ordinary employee of the G.W.R. (an engine driver or signalman) would have been lucky to have earned much more than £1 a week.

HONOURS

In *The Lives of the Engineers* (1862) Samuel Smiles listed the honours heaped on Robert Stephenson:

> In 1847 he entered the House of Commons for Whitby . . . he was made Knight of the Order of Leopold [by the Belgian King] . . . was decorated with the Grand Cross of the Order of St. Olaf [by the King of Sweden] . . . the Emperor of France decorated him with the Legion of Honour . . . the University of Oxford made him a Doctor of Civil Laws. In 1856 he was elected President of the Institute of Civil Engineers . . .

Rivalry and Friendship

Robert Stephenson (1803-1859) and Isambard Kingdom Brunel (1806-1859) were Britain's greatest engineers for the first 20 years of Victoria's reign. They were both friends and rivals.

THE ENGINEERS COMPARED

The great Victorian biographer, Samuel Smiles, pointed out in his *Lives of the Engineers* (1862) some of the differences between the Stephensons and Brunels.

> Both men were the sons of distinguished men, and both inherited the fame and followed in the footsteps of their fathers. The Stephensons were inventive, practical, and sagacious; the Brunels ingenious, imaginative and daring. The former were as thoroughly English in their characteristics as the latter perhaps were as thoroughly French. The fathers and the sons were alike successful in their works . . . [however] measured by practical and profitable results, the Stephensons were undoubtedly the safer men to follow.

What did Stephenson and Brunel have in common and in what ways did they differ? Why, do you think, does the author come to the conclusion that "the Stephensons were undoubtedly the safer men to follow"?

Robert Stephenson.

Isambard Kingdom Brunel.

THE BATTLE OF THE GAUGES

Brunel and Stephenson were to disagree with each other on several occasions. Smiles tells us about one clash.

> Their respective railway districts "marched" with each other, and it became their business to invade or defend those districts, according to the policy that their respective boards [of directors] might direct. The gauge fixed on by Mr. Brunel for the Great Western Railway [7 feet], so entirely different from that adopted by the Stephensons on the Northern and Midland lines [4 feet 8½ inches], was from the first a cause of great contention. But Mr. Brunel had always an aversion to follow any man's lead . . . . Robert Stephenson . . . though less bold, was more practical, preferring to follow the old routes . . .

The struggle between Brunel and Stephenson over which gauge would become standard was settled by Parliament in 1846 in favour of the "narrow gauge" of 4 feet 8½ inches. Why do you think Parliament decided it would be foolish to have more than one railway gauge in Britain?

OCCASIONAL MEETINGS

This rivalry did not prevent Stephenson and Brunel from meeting each other. Brunel recorded in his diary on 5 May 1846:

> I am just returned from spending an evening with Robert Stephenson. It is very delightful in the midst of our incessant personal professional contests, carried to the extreme limit of fair opposition, to meet him on a perfectly friendly footing and discuss engineering points . . .

Consult a biography of Brunel or Stephenson to find out why the rivalry between the two engineers was particularly acute in the 1840s.

COLLABORATION

On more than one occasion the two great men gave each other practical help. Isambard Brunel, in his *Life of I.K. Brunel* described one such occasion in 1849.

> Mr. Brunel had previously taken part in operations of this nature. When Mr. Robert Stephenson was about to undertake the floating of the tubes of the Conway and Britannia Bridges, he asked his friends Mr. Brunel and Mr. Locke to give him their assistance. They were present at all, or nearly all, these difficult operations and Mr. Brunel had an active share in the work . . .

1859

Brunel and Stephenson died in the same year. The President of the Institution of Civil Engineers, Joseph Locke, spoke for many when he said of the two engineers:

> Their lives and labours . . . are before us; and it will be our own fault if we fail to draw from them useful lessons for our guidance . . . . We, at least, who are benefited by their successes . . . have a duty to perform; and that duty is, to honour their memory and emulate their example.

Isambard Kingdom Brunel owes his great reputation as an engineer in part to his extraordinary skill as a bridge-builder. Most of his bridges were built for railway companies and most can be found in southern and south-western England. Of the two bridges dealt with here, one was begun at the start and the other at the end of Brunel's career.

CLIFTON SUSPENSION BRIDGE

Murray's *Handbook to Gloucester, Hereford and Worcester* (1872), described Brunel's bridge across the Avon, near Bristol.

At the spot where the passage is deepest and most picturesque is a chain suspension bridge, having a span of 703 feet at a height of 245 feet, with 30 feet of roadway and a length of 220 feet, the carriage way being 20 feet and the footways 5½ feet wide. The bridge hangs from the chains by rods 2 inches in diameter and 8 feet apart, 81 on each

Brunel's plans for the Clifton Bridge. Engineers often drew up several schemes from which their clients could choose. Cost was usually the factor that decided the matter. Plan "B" was chosen in this

FINANCIAL DIFFICULTIES

Although he was a great engineer, many of Brunel's plans were to run into financial problems. The Clifton Bridge, begun in 1836, was not completed until 1864, five years after Brunel's death. This extract is from I. Brunel's *The Life of I.K. Brunel* (1870).

The works were commenced by the Leigh abutment, which was completed in 1840 . . . [However] in 1843 the whole of the funds raised [amounting to £45,000] were exhausted, and there still remained to be executed the

side of the structure . . . . The chains are secured by solid masonry in chambers 75 feet below the level of the bridge . . .

Why do you think Brunel built the bridge at this particular spot? The bridge was built for road traffic and is still used today.

case (but the lions were never put on the top of the piers – see the colour illustration on the front cover of this book).

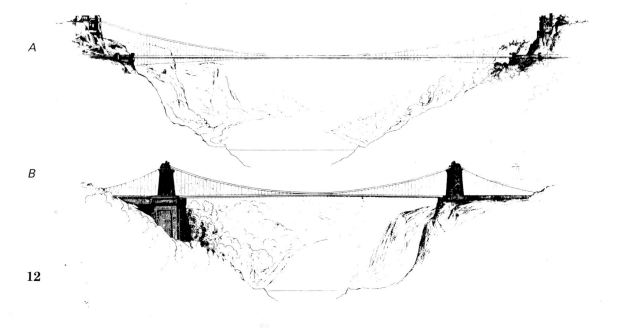

A

B

ornamental additions to the piers [the cost of which was estimated about £4,000], half of the iron work, the suspension of the chain and rods, the construction of the flooring, and the completion of the approaches etc., the estimate for the execution of which was £30,000.

Try to identify on Brunel's plan the "piers" and the Leigh "abutment". Why do you think that the "ornamental additions to the piers" were never built?

BRIDGE OVER THE TAMAR

The *Plymouth, Devonport and Stonehouse Herald* of Saturday, 7 May 1859 carried a report on the Royal Albert Bridge (which it described as "one of the greatest mechanised enterprises of the present or past ages"), opened a few days before by Prince Albert.

To cross the Tamar with one unsupported span nearly a quarter of a mile in length was, of course, impossible, and Mr. Brunel had not only to make his pier in the centre of the river, but, having no place to which to secure the tension chains on which the roadway [i.e. where the railway track lay] hung, had also to contrive to make them in a manner perfectly self-supporting. For this the suspension chains hang down from the piers in a segment of a circle, and are bolted to the roadway, while above the roadway, so as to form the other segment of the circle, are two monstrous tubes of arched wrought iron, connected with the ends of the chains, and which precisely answer the purpose of metal bows. The tubes and tension chains being connected with iron trusses and both fastened to the roadway, the whole acts as a double bow. As the tension chains give under a strain, they straighten down the bow above them, and so the ends of the chains are supported and kept in place, while the deflections of the tubes themselves in turn relieve the roadway.

You should read this description of the Royal Albert Bridge in conjunction with the picture of the bridge.

The Royal Albert Bridge. The central column, standing on a masonry pier, was built of cast iron; the trusses (arches) were of wrought iron. Why, do you think, was this? Note that there is plenty of clearance for tall-masted ships – why would this have been so important with this particular bridge?

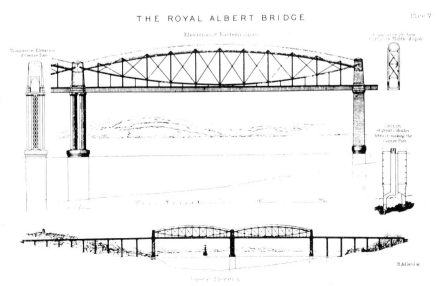

THE ROYAL ALBERT BRIDGE

Stephenson's Bridges

Robert Stephenson was an important railway engineer but is even better known as a bridge-builder.

THE HIGH-LEVEL BRIDGE

The Newcastle high-level bridge was begun in 1846 and completed in three years. Built of cast iron, it still carries road and rail traffic on its two decks. In 1858 the *Quarterly Review* pointed out:

> The problem was to throw a railway bridge across the deep ravine which lies between the towns of Newcastle and Gateshead, at the bottom of which flows the Tyne . . . the breadth of the river at the point of crossing is 515 feet. The first difficulty encountered in building the bridge was in securing a solid foundation for the piers. The dimensions of the piles to be driven were so huge, that Stephenson called Nasmyth's Titanic steam hammer to his aid . . . the first pile was driven . . . to a depth of 32 feet in four minutes. Two hammers of 30 cwt each were kept in regular use, making from 60 to 70 strokes per minute . . .

This was the first time a steam hammer was used in bridge-building. Try to find out what method of sinking piles was used before this.

A TUBULAR FORM OF BRIDGE

The greatest difficulty in building the Chester and Holyhead Railway in the 1840s was crossing the Menai Straits, separating Anglesey from mainland Wales. The bridge had to span a width of 1100 feet, be high enough to allow sea-going vessels to pass underneath and be strong enough to withstand a daily rise and fall of the tide of 25 feet. John Timbs in his *History of Wonderful Inventions* (1867) described the solution to the problem.

> When Mr. Robert Stephenson . . . proposed to span the Menai Straits by a tunnel of wrought iron stretching from side to side, and allowing a passage for the trains to run through its interior, he confided the experiment to be made

THE ROYAL BORDER BRIDGE

This extract is taken from Thomas Dugdale's guide book to England and Wales, published in the 1860s.

> The new railway viaduct across the Tweed at Berwick opened by Her Majesty on her way to Scotland [29 August 1850], is an outstanding triumph of modern engineering. . . . From its length of 2,170 feet, and its height, 125 feet, this is the largest stone viaduct in the world. . . . The whole contains upward of one million cubic feet of masonry, and in the inner portions of the arches two millions and a half of bricks.

Look at an atlas to find out what two other natural obstacles between Edinburgh and Dundee had to be crossed by railway bridges before the Queen would be able to go directly to Balmoral.

The High Level Bridge at Newcastle. Note the train crossing the bridge. Can you think of any reason why the road ran below and not above the railway lines?

upon the strength of the iron for that purpose to Mr. Fairbairn, the eminent engineer of Manchester, who introduced wrought iron girders . . . . After many experiments it was proposed to build an iron box, 460 feet long, 30 feet high, and 14 feet broad, on the banks of the Menai Straits; to float this mass of 3,450 tons at high water to openings in piers for its reception; to lift it upwards of 100 feet and build solid masonry underneath for its support . . .

Find out what are the differences between wrought and cast iron. Why was cast iron less suitable for bridge-building?

Floating the second tube of the Britannia Tubular Bridge in 1849. In 1970 the tubes were badly damaged by fire and the rebuilding of the bridge has altered its appearance.

THE BRITANNIA BRIDGE – FACTS AND FIGURES

1. Total length of each tube .	1,492	feet
2. Total length of tubes	2,984	”
3. Greatest height of bridge above high water mark . .	240	”
4. Height of the bottom of the bridge above high water mark	104	”
5. Quantity of masonry in piers, abutments and wing walls	1,400,000	cu.feet
6. Timber used in scaffolding	450,000	”
7. Weight of wrought iron in the tubes	10,000	tons
8. Weight of cast iron in the tubes	1,400	”
9. Weight of one of the 2 tubes	5,000	”
10. Cost of one of the 2 tubes .	£54,000	
11. Cost of the scaffolding . . .	£50,000	
12. Cost of whole bridge	£500,000	

Building Tunnels

By 1863 80 miles of railway tunnel had been built in Britain. A newspaper report in 1984 showed how well these tunnels had been built. A train pulling oil tankers exploded and burned for several days in the Summit Tunnel under the Pennines near Littleborough in Yorkshire. This 2885-yard tunnel on the Manchester and Bradford lines was built in 1859 by Stephenson. In the worst affected areas the brickwork was damaged in only two out of six courses. The tunnel was re-opened in August 1985.

ECONOMY IS THE PRINCIPAL TEST

In Our Iron Roads (1857) F.S. Williams explained why tunnels were built.

> In the construction of a railway . . . it is usually found that some portion of the earth rises to such a height that it is best to conduct the line underground . . . it is a rule . . . that to make a cutting more than 60 feet deep would be costlier than to "bore" [i.e. to tunnel] unless the material is required for a neighbouring embankment. Economy is the principal test in these matters. . .

The railway engineer's main task was to build a line that was as level and as direct as possible. Why do you think this was?

CONSTRUCTING A TUNNEL

The author of "Difficulties of Railway Engineering" in the Quarterly Review of 1858 outlined the procedure followed in building a tunnel.

> To test the character of the underground strata . . . vertical borings are made through the site of the proposed tunnel . . . . In some cases, where the tunnel is of no great extent, a driftway [i.e. a tunnel] is dug through its whole length . . . [but more usually] the tunnel is commenced at various points, by means of vertical working shafts . . . . Excavating, followed by building in of the brick or stone work of the tunnel, proceeds . . . each way, the excavated stuff being drawn up the shaft by means of a horse gin, or by steam power. The tunnel is usually worked in lengths of about 20 feet, and arched with brick or stone from eighteen inches to two feet in thickness. By this method a large number of short tunnels are formed . . . [and] are ultimately united into one, and a vast body of men can be employed without confusion at the same time.

Horse gins in action at the Box Tunnel on the G.W.R. (completed in 1841).

THE LONGEST TUNNEL

The Severn Tunnel was first suggested in 1865. However, work did not start until 1873 and the tunnel was not opened until 1886. We can follow in D. Gooch's diary (he was by now Chairman of the G.W.R.) the problems the engineers faced.

> Oct. 17th 1879 . . . Yesterday we struck a strong feeder of water in the heading under the land on the Welsh side, which is more than our pumps can

THE THAMES TUNNEL

The world's first sub-aqueous (under-water) tunnel was built under the Thames between Wapping and Rotherhithe by Marc Brunel. In *The Land We Live In*, Vol. II, published in the 1850s, the author detailed the struggle to build the tunnel.

> A company was formed in 1824 . . . it was not until 1842 that the tunnel was finished . . . . The Thames water ran into the tunnel, and the money ran out of the company's coffers, at an equally fearful rate . . . . In 1826, the works were commenced; in September . . . the river broke through . . . into the excavations; in October [1826] it did so for a second time; in May 1827, it so completely overwhelmed the tunnel as to stop the works for three months. But the sad calamity occurred on August 12th 1828, when the river burst in with awful force and destroyed the working machinery, drowned six men . . . for seven long years the works were suspended . . .

The tunnel, built for foot passengers, was finally opened in 1843 but it was never a financial success. In 1865 it was converted to railway use and is now part of the London Underground.

manage . . . . Oct. 10th 1883. The large spring that broke out in the Severn Tunnel a couple of years ago broke out in a fresh place today . . . flooding the tunnel, and a couple of days afterwards the tide rose in the Severn, covering the land and getting down one of our shafts . . . one man was drowned. So high a tide has not been known for 100 years. Oct. 27th 1884 . . . The spring is now about 7,000 gallons per minute, but is fully under the control of the pumps . . . Saturday Sept. 5th, 1885. I took a special train through the Severn Tunnel . . . [it] is a big work and has been a source of great anxiety to me. It will be some months yet before we can open to the public as the permanent pumping . . . machinery has to be arranged and fixed. The Severn Tunnel is 4½ miles long and 76 million bricks were used in its construction.

The Thames Tunnel as it appeared when originally opened for traffic.

Building the Cornwall Railway

In 1841 there were about 1800 miles of railway in the United Kingdom. By 1851 this had risen to nearly 7000 miles, and by 1871 to over 15,000 miles. A small fraction of the 1871 total was accounted for by the 65½ miles of the Cornwall Railway which ran from Plymouth to Falmouth. Construction of the line, under Brunel's supervision, began in 1852 and the line was opened in 1859.

DIFFICULT COUNTRY

The problems facing Brunel in building this line are explained by his son in *The Life of Isambard Kingdom Brunel* (1870):

> The district through which the line passes is very deficient in the materials requisite for the construction of a railway . . . .
>
> In consequence of the number of valleys that the railway had to cross, the aggregate lengths of the viaducts, thirty-four in number, exclusive of the Saltash bridge [i.e. the Royal Albert Bridge] is upwards of four miles on a line of sixty miles.

Brunel built the viaducts with masonry piers supporting timber superstructures. Why do you think he adopted this technique?

The Moorswater Viaduct, one mile from Liskeard. Note the piers from the original Brunel viaduct.

THE OPENING OF THE LINE

The *Cornish Telegraph* had a reporter on the train from Truro to Plymouth on the day in May 1859 Prince Albert opened the line. It was a frustrating journey as the newspaper report made clear.

> We learn that the progress of the train from Truro with a great number of visitors eager to participate in the interesting ceremonies of the day, was everything that could be wished till its arrival at Liskeard, when the engine came to a dead lock. "The Argo" [the engine], says our reporter on the train, "is twelve years old, and had lately done much work." . . . engine-doctors felt the patient's pulse, and with wrenches and tools are prescribing for him; but the case is believed to be hopeless . . . . Plymouth is telegraphed for an engine, and before steam can be got up and the new fire horse can reach us, two precious hours are consumed. At last the new steed comes . . . at express speed we soon reach St. Germans . . .

The Truro party in the end arrived just in time to see Prince Albert. Why do you think the reporter talks about "engine-doctors" and calls the engine "a steed"?

THE VIADUCTS AT LISKEARD

Guide books of the time usually drew the attention of travellers to some of the more spectacular viaducts on the line. *Murray's Hand-Book to Devon and Cornwall* (1872) describes the viaducts just outside Liskeard:

> **Left of the station is the eminence of Clicker Tor [a rocky hill] . . . its jagged rocks protruding from the fern and turf . . . on each side of the tor the railway crosses a valley by a lofty viaduct, and on the Plymouth side by the most ornamental on the whole line. It is a beautiful piece of woodwork, and a most picturesque object in connection with the richly wooded valley it spans.**

REPLACING THE SOUTH CORNWALL VIADUCTS

P.J. Margary was the engineer responsible for the Plymouth-Falmouth line. The viaducts were a constant worry to him. In 1883 Margary reported to the directors:

> **All the viaducts are maintained in the same general state of repair as far as the soundness of the timber is concerned, the practice being to send gangs of men to each viaduct in turn to examine and change every defective piece of timber . . . . [However] on some of the viaducts there is either a curve or an inherent weakness in the original structure and in these there has been a distortion in the shape of the timber superstructure, necessitating the introduction of numerous shores . . . These renewals were made piece by piece under circumstances of considerable difficulty with the traffic going over the viaducts while the renewals are taking place . . .**

Rebuilding a viaduct on the Cornwall Railway in the later nineteenth century. Compare this with the photograph of the Moorswater viaduct today. Note how stone or brick arches were made and also the Brunel wooden viaduct in the background.

What do you think Margary advised the directors to do? Look again at the photograph of the Moorswater Viaduct. (Why do you think it has two sets of piers?)

Ships: from Paddle Steamer

Until the development of the compound engine in the 1860s steam merchant vessels could not compete with sailing ships except for short journeys. However, steam ships which carried a light cargo, like passengers and mail, were developed before 1860.

THE *GREAT WESTERN* AND THE *SIRIUS*

Early steam ships were built of wood and propelled through the water by rotating paddles on either side in the middle of the vessel. Brunel's son described the race between his father's first ship and the *Sirius* to see which could cross the Atlantic most quickly using steam power.

> The 'Great Western' started on her first voyage to New York on Sunday April 8th at 10.0 a.m. . . . . She arrived at New York at 2.0 p.m. on Monday, 23rd having consumed three-fourths of the coal she had taken on board.
>
> She found that the 'Sirius' had arrived before her; but under the circumstances the palm [i.e. the prize] was due to the 'Great Western' for the 'Sirius' had left Cork eight hours before the 'Great Western' left Bristol . . . and had only arrived at New York on the morning of the day in the afternoon of which the 'Great Western' came in, and, what is after all the most important point for comparison, the 'Great Western' had nearly 200 tons of coal left, while the 'Sirius' not only consumed all her coal but also all the combustible articles which could possibly be thrown on the fire, including . . . a child's doll! (*The Life of Isambard Kingdom Brunel*)

What advantage had the *Sirius* in leaving from Cork? Calculate how much coal the *Great Western* carried for the voyage across the Atlantic.

THE *GREAT BRITAIN*

D. Gooch, the great locomotive engineer of the Great Western Railway, noted in his *Memoirs and Diary*:

> On the 11th December (1844) the Great Britain steamship was ready for trial and I went down to Bristol to go out to sea with her. When she entered the lock leading into the river she caught the stern works on each side and could not get through . . . . She was . . . got free . . . and the lock walls were lowered, and we got out the next time . . . . She soon after began her voyages to America . . . and after a few voyages was run aground . . . on the coast of Ireland . . . . She was a heavy loss to her shareholders, as she was then sold to Messrs Gibbs of Liverpool for a very small sum. They took her engines out [and put new ones in] and she has since been employed profitably in the Australian trade [for this the ship was also equipped with masts and sails].

The *Great Britain* was one of the first ships which used screw propulsion (invented in the 1830s by Francis Pettit Smith and John Ericsson) rather than paddle wheels. The screw, a shaft with blades, propelled the ship by revolving rapidly under water at the rear of the ship. It was more economical in its use of fuel and less vulnerable to wave damage than paddle wheels. If you live near Bristol try to visit the *Great Britain* which is preserved there.

Brunel's three great ships in profile. ▷ Can you identify each one?

to Compound Engine □□□□□□□□□□□□□□

COMPOUND ENGINES

The great defect of the *Great Eastern* lay in Brunel's under-estimation of the coal required to fuel her single cylinder 6600 h.p. engines. The steam produced could only be used once and, therefore, most of the energy was wasted. By the end of the 1850s compound engines (which used the steam twice) were being developed which reduced coal consumption by 60 per cent. In the 1880s triple expansion engines were introduced (they used the steam three times over). In 1887 the scientist Lyon Playfair noted:

Not long since a steamer of 3,000 tons going on a long voyage might require 2,200 tons of coal, and carry only a limited cargo of 800 tons. Now, a modern steamer will take the same voyage with 800 tons of coal, and carry a freight of 2,200 tons. While coal has thus been economised, human labour has been lowered. In 1870 it required 47 hands on board our steamships for every 100 tons of capacity. Now only 28 are necessary. (Quoted in W.H.B. Court, *British Economic History 1870-1914*, 1965)

There is a picture of a triple expansion engine on page 5.

It was not until 1883 that Britain had more steam than sail vessels and even in 1901 sailing ships accounted for nearly a quarter of the British merchant fleet.

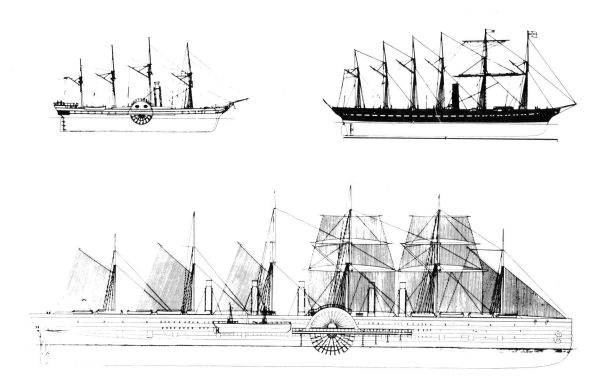

Ships: from Wood to Steel

Not until 1870 were more iron ships built in Britain than wooden ones. By 1880 only small sailing vessels were being built of wood and by the end of Victoria's reign iron ships had given way to vessels made of steel.

THE MERITS OF IRON

William Fairbairn, the great experimental engineer, made clear the advantages of iron ships in his *Treatise of Iron Shipbuilding, its History and Progress* (1865).

> The iron ship in lightness, durability and capacity of cargo, is infinitely superior to a vessel built of wood; and if properly constructed and carefully looked after, will last more than double the time of vessels composed of the best teak and English oak . . . the superior strength of the iron ship ensures greatly increased security to the owners and . . . to the crew and passengers . . . . As regards cargo, there is less risk from damage, as the iron ship is . . . perfectly water tight and free from . . . that creaking motion observable in the joints of a wooden vessel plunging in a heavy sea . . . [and] in the iron ship the enlargement of the interior is so great as to enable the vessel to carry from $1/8$ to $1/10$ more cargo . . . than a vessel built of wood . . .

Why do you think that steam power and wooden-built ships did not go well together? Many people believed that iron ships would be too heavy to float and that compasses would not work in vessels built of iron.

Notice the large amount of space taken up by the engines. What three sources of power could the ship use?

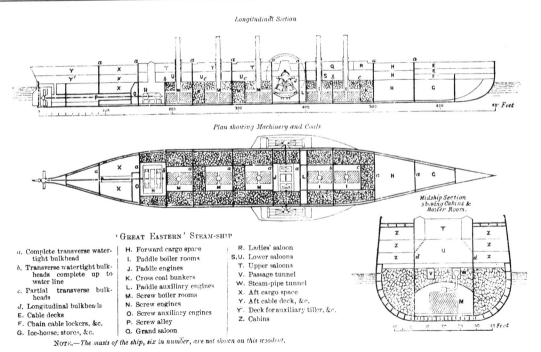

Longitudinal Section

Plan showing Machinery and Coals

Midship Section showing Cabins & Boiler Room.

'GREAT EASTERN' STEAM-SHIP

a. Complete transverse water-tight bulkhead
b. Transverse watertight bulk-heads complete up to water line
c. Partial transverse bulk-heads
d. Longitudinal bulkheads
E. Cable decks
F. Chain cable lockers, &c.
G. Ice-house, stores, &c.

H. Forward cargo space
I. Paddle boiler rooms
J. Paddle engines
K. Cross coal bunkers
L. Paddle auxiliary engines
M. Screw boiler rooms
N. Screw engines
O. Screw auxiliary engines
P. Screw alley
Q. Grand saloon

R. Ladies' saloon
S,U. Lower saloons
T. Upper saloons
V. Passage tunnel
W. Steam-pipe tunnel
X. Aft cargo space
Y. Aft cable deck, &c.
Y'. Deck for auxiliary tiller, &c.
Z. Cabins

NOTE.—The masts of the ship, six in number, are not shown on this woodcut.

AGROUND ON THE IRISH COAST

The world's first really large iron ship, Brunel's *Great Britain*, suffered an unfortunate accident on its second voyage to New York. *Cassell's Illustrated History of England* (1873) tells the story:

> She left Liverpool on 22nd September 1846, and within 10 hours struck on the Irish coast . . . it was not until August 1847 that she was at length got again into the water . . . . For a whole winter . . . the 'Great Britain' was exposed to the action of heavy seas beating her upon the sands and rocks of Dundrum Bay, and she went through this ordeal without suffering any serious damage in her hull or in any other part. A vessel of wood could not have survived . . . which only confirmed the scientific experiments of Professor Hodgkinson, who showed that the comparative resistance of wrought iron to a direct crushing force is more than seven times as great as that of the best British oak.

You will understand now what Fairbairn meant when he talked about the "durability" of iron. So durable has the *Great Britain* been that today you can visit her at Bristol.

"THE CRYSTAL PALACE OF THE SEA"

Built in the early 1850s Brunel's *Great Eastern* was nearly six times as large as the *Great Britain*. It was estimated in 1858 that she could be fitted up to carry comfortably 10,000 people. No bigger ship was built anywhere in the world until 1901. Brunel's son described the ship.

> . . . 680 feet long, 83 feet wide, and 58 feet deep. Her gross tonnage is 18,915 tons. She is divided into water-tight compartments by ten bulkheads . . . in addition there are partial bulkheads, which form the ends of coal bunkers [and] aid materially in strengthening the flat bottom of the ship . . . the bottom is made double . . . . Mr. Brunel considered that the double skin would greatly diminish the chance of such an accident occurring as would cause any of the compartments to be filled with water . . . (*The Life of Isambard Kingdom Brunel*)

Try to find out more about this ship's career. She was a commercial failure but important in an engineering sense.

SHIPS MADE OF STEEL

In 1888 the *Journal of the Iron and Steel Institute* commented on the speed with which steel had taken over from iron in shipbuilding.

> Between 1866 and 1876 only three small ships were built of steel in the United Kingdom . . . . Mr. Parker, Chief Engineer to Lloyds Registry, states that in 1878 the quantity of steel used for steamships was only 2,682 tons against 243,717 tons of iron; but in 1887, 195,907 tons of steel were used for steamships, 14,333 tons for sailing vessels, and only 24,052 tons of iron for steamers and 28,150 tons for sailing ships . . . by the introduction of steel, superior ships have been built, capable of carrying 4 per cent more cargo, on a consumption of 25 per cent less coal.
>
> The cost of steel ships . . . is not more, their strength is greater . . .

Note that sailing ships were still being built towards the end of Queen Victoria's reign. What qualities does steel have which iron lacks and why are there differences between these two metals? The information on page 34 will help you with this question.

Mechanical Engineering

Many new and important machines were invented by British engineers during the period 1837 – 1901. These machines, in turn, made possible the engineering triumph of the bridge-, railway- and ship-builders.

THE STEAM HAMMER

James Nasmyth in his *Autobiography* (1883) explained the working of his first steam hammer in 1839:

> My steam hammer . . . consisted of, first a massive anvil on which to rest the work; second, a block of iron constituting the hammer . . .; and third, an inverted steam cylinder to whose piston rod the hammer block was attached. All that was then required to produce a most effective hammer was simply to admit steam of sufficient pressure into the cylinder, so as to act on the under-side of the piston, and thus to raise the hammer-block attached to the end of the piston-rod. By a very simple arrangement of a slide valve, under the control of an attendant, the steam was allowed to escape, and thus permit the massive block of iron rapidly to descend by its own gravity upon the work then upon the anvil.

The illustration of a steam hammer gives a clear idea of the size they had reached by the 1870s. For what purpose do you think they were used in the iron and steel industry?

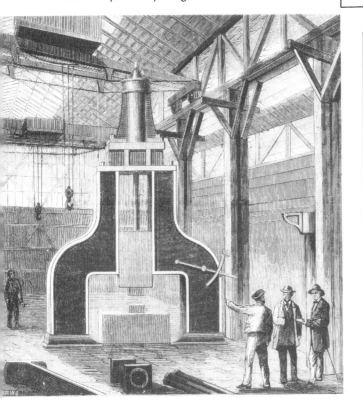

Nasmyth's steam hammer. The head on this hammer probably weighed 20 tons.

THE RIVETING MACHINE

> To facilitate the manufacture of iron-sided ships, Mr. Fairbairn, about the year 1839, invented a machine for riveting boiler plates by steam power. The usual method by which this process had before been executed was by hand-hammers, worked by men placed at each side of the plate to be riveted . . . . But this process was tedious and expensive, as well as clumsy and imperfect, and some more rapid and precise method of fixing the plates firmly together was urgently wanted. Mr. Fairbairn's machine completely supplied the want. (S. Smiles, *Industrial Biography*, 1863).

Why do you think the author seems to be unsure when precisely this machine was invented?

ACCURACY

In 1856 Joseph Whitworth described his micrometer to a meeting of the Institute of Mechanical Engineers held at Glasgow:

> I have brought with me for your inspection a small machine by which a difference in length of one-millionth part of an inch is at once detected. The principle employed is that of employing the sense of touch instead of sight . . . we find, in practice in the workshop, that it is easier to work to the ten-thousandth of an inch . . . by the help of the new machine, than to the one-hundredth of an inch from the lines on a two foot rule.

Ask your science teacher to show you a micrometer.

OPPOSITION TO NEW MACHINES

As you might expect not everyone welcomed the introduction of new machines. The file-cutters of Sheffield in the early 1860s were very angry at the threat to their jobs posed by a file-cutting machine (based on Nasmyth's steam hammer). One of them wrote this poem:

> It's the wonder of wonders, is this
>   mighty steam hammer,
> What folks say it will do, it would make
>   anyone stammer;
> They say it will cut files as fast as three
>   men and a lad,
> But two out of three, it's a fact, they are
>   bad.
>
> So unite well together, by good moral
>   means,
> Don't be intimidated by these infernal
>   machines;
> Let them boast as they will – and
>   though the press clamour,
> After all, lads, there's nothing like
>   wrist, chisel and hammer.

(Quoted in H. Pawson and J. Brailsford, *Illustrated Guide to Sheffield and Its Neighbourhood*, 1862)

A side view of the great hydraulic press used in raising the Britannia Tubular Bridge. One of these machines (invented by Joseph Bramah, 1748-1814) was estimated to be capable of lifting as many as 30,000 men.

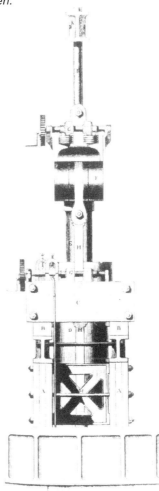

Building Locomotives

In the early years of the nineteenth century railway locomotives were crude machines. However, by 1850 the steam locomotive had become much more sophisticated – it was fast, reliable, powerful and showing most of the features that locomotives were to retain until the end of the steam age.

DANIEL GOOCH

Gooch (1816-1889) was the leading locomotive engineer in the mid-nineteenth century.

> **In 1837 . . . he was appointed superintendent of the Great Western Railway on the recommendation of Marc Isambard Brunel [Isambard Kingdom Brunel's father]. He held this post for 27 years. Gooch took advantage of the space allowed by the broad gauge . . . to design locomotives on boldly original lines. His engines achieved a speed and safety not previously deemed possible, and not exceeded since . . .** (*Dictionary of National Biography*, 1893)

How old was Gooch when he was appointed to his post at the G.W.R.? Could someone of this age get a post of similar responsibility today?

"Lord of the Isles". Does the lack of a covered cab suggest that the G.W.R. did not regard their engine drivers as very important?

THE *LORD OF THE ISLES*

One of the G.W.R.'s locomotives was exhibited at the Great Exhibition in 1851. The following year George Meason in his *Illustrated Guide to the Great Western Railway* described this engine:

> **The 'Lord of the Isles' . . . a noble engine on eight wheels . . . is capable of taking a passenger-train of 120 tons, at an average speed of sixty miles an hour; and its effective power . . . is equal to that of 740 horses. Its weight . . . amounts to thirty-five tons, independently of the tender, which, when laden [with coke], weighs nearly eighteen more. Its cylinder has a diameter of eighteen, and the piston a stroke of twenty-four inches, while the driving wheel is eight feet in diameter, and the maximum pressure of steam equal to 120lb on the square inch. The consumption of coke, with a load of twenty tons, travelling thirty miles an hour, amounts to 20lb per mile.**

Study the picture of Gooch's engine, the *Lord of the Isles* carefully and relate it to Meason's description. The engine took its name from a poem by Sir Walter Scott which dealt with Robert Bruce, the Scottish leader, who defeated the English at Bannockburn in 1314.

JOURNEY TIMES: 1845 AND 1985

In 1843 the average speed of the G.W.R. was 33 m.p.h. Thanks to Gooch there were rapid improvements and between 1845 – 1848 two engines designed by him achieved speeds of 70 m.p.h.

Distance (miles)	Station	Exeter Express (1845)	Inter-City 125 (1985)
0	Paddington	09.30	09.05
53	Didcot	10.43	–
77	Swindon	11.20	09.58
107	Bath	12.10	10.20
118	Bristol	12.30	10.37

How long did the journey from Paddington to Bristol take in 1845 and in 1985? Can you calculate the average speed of the trains?

The Engineer *magazine said that Ritchie's new locomotive engine of 1856 "appears to possess several advantages in combination with many faults". What differences can you see between this odd-looking engine and the "Lord of the Isles"?*

THE LOCOMOTIVE WORKS

All the large railway companies in Victoria's reign had their own workshops. This extract from *Old and New London*, published about 1880, describes the Stratford (East London) depot of the Great Eastern Railway.

The works which were established here about 1847 cover a large extent of ground, and give employment to upwards of 2,500 hands . . . . The machinery throughout is of the most perfect description . . . one shop contains upwards of 100 machines for the performance of the most delicate work . . . we may state that about 500 engines, 3,000 carriages and 10,000 waggons are here kept in constant repair . . .

Today railway workshops in the North-East are being closed. Why do we not talk about employees as "hands" today?

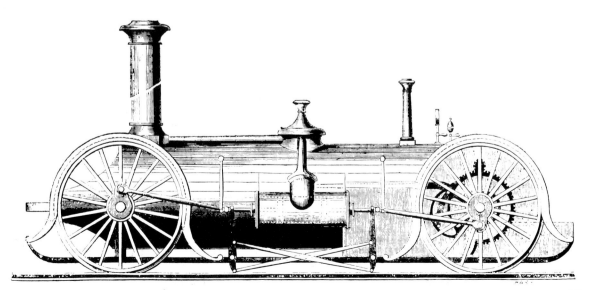

Engineering and Agriculture

Before the 1830s machinery played very little part in British agriculture. This was all to change during Victoria's reign. Food output doubled in the nineteenth century, partly due to the introduction of machinery into the countryside.

FARM MACHINERY AT THE GREAT EXHIBITION

Busby W., U.K., 2 or 4 horse plough, horse-hoe on the ridge, ribbing corn drill, and cart.

Crosskill W., U.K., Norwegian harrow, meal mill, cart, clod crusher, and gorse bruiser.

Garrett & Sons, U.K., horse hoe, general purpose drill, four-row turnip drill on the flat, improved hand barrow drill for grass seeds, steam engine and thrashing machine.

Hornsby and Sons, U.K., corn and seed drill, two-row turnip drill on the ridge, oil cake bruiser, steam engine.

McCormick, C.H., United States, reaping machine.

List all the machines mentioned in this extract. (A drill is a machine for planting seeds at regular intervals.) "The first place among the agricultural machinery in the Crystal Palace," said the *Illustrated Exhibitor*, "must be accorded to our cousins from the other side of the Atlantic." Can you think of any reasons why farmers in the U.S.A. used more machines than British farmers did? What machine today is the equivalent (and more) of McCormick's reaper?

E. R. & F. TURNER'S
IMPROVED
PRIZE THRASHING MACHINES

ADVERTISEMENTS.

HAVE BEEN AWARDED

THE SILVER MEDAL OF THE R.A.S., ENGLAND, AT CANTERBURY, 1860;
SILVER MEDAL OF THE AGRICULTURAL SOCIETY OF EAST FLANDERS, AT GHENT, 1861;
SILVER MEDAL OF THE INTERNATIONAL EXHIBITION, AT LILLE, 1863;
FIRST PRIZE OF THE AGRICULTURAL SOCIETY OF EAST BELGIUM, AT LIEGE, 1863;
LARGE SILVER MEDAL AT HAMBURG, 1863; GOLD MEDAL OF THE R.A.S. OF HOLLAND, 1863;
SILVER MEDAL OF THE INTERNATIONAL EXHIBITION, AT COLOGNE, 1865;
GOLD MEDAL OP THE R.A.S. OF BRABANT, AT BRUSSELS, 1868;
FIRST CLASS SILVER MEDAL AT ALTONA, 1869;
GOLD MEDAL AT THE HAGUE, SEPTEMBER, 1872, &c.

The following important advantages claimed for these Machines will be esteemed by all practical men :—
The Wrought Iron Tension Braces fitted in all the larger Machines secure **increased strength with less weight.**
The Diminished height of the platform saves labour, ensures steadiness in work, and increases the durability of the Machine.
An efficient and ready means of adjustment for the Drum Bearing Brasses of the larger Machines.
A simple and efficient Chaff Elevator, which can be attached at a slightly increased cost.
The frameworks are constructed of thoroughly sound and well-seasoned timber, and so well stayed that wrenching is effectually prevented. By this means durability is increased and the various bearings kept level.
The various separations are effected in the most perfect manner, and are delivered in the most convenient places for removal.
The use of patent spring hangers where practicable, the steadiness of the Machine being thereby increased and economy in oil effected.
The vibrating parts of the Machine being balanced, reduces the strain on the framework.
The cup elevators attached to these Machines are certain in action, whether the grain is dry or damp, and they are superior to the blast elevator when the corn is brittle or tender, as breakage of the grain is avoided.
The ease with which they may be taken to pieces when repairs are necessary.
The addition of the patent adjustable screen is recommended, as by its means the quantity of tail corn may be regulated at pleasure to suit the varying kinds of grain.

Many firms making agricultural machinery sprang up between 1840 and 1860. Knights' Country Handbook and Suffolk Almanac *(1875) contains many such advertisements. What are the two ways in which the advertisement tries to sell the machine. Consult a nineteenth-century handbook for your area. Does it contain similar advertisements and do these firms still exist today?*

TRADITIONAL RURAL SKILLS

Even at the end of Victoria's reign many farming tasks still relied on horse or human muscle power. Reaping (or mowing) machines still had not entirely replaced the scythe. In *Hills and the Seas* (1906), Hilaire Belloc described how as a young man he had mowed a field by hand.

When I got out into the long grass the sun was not yet risen . . . I went forward over the field cutting lane after lane through the grass . . . . At the end of every lane, I sharpened my scythe and looked back at the work done, and then carried my scythe down again upon my

14 h.p. double-cylinder ploughing engine, 1858 (Messrs. J. Fowler & Co., Steam Plough Works, Leeds).

"I sing of Fowler's famed steam plough –
Prodigious imp of modern birth,
What mortal lungs can shout thy worth!"
(Anon., mid-nineteenth century)

_____STEAM POWER ON THE FARM_____

In 1901 there were nearly 9000 (mainly portable) steam engines servicing 300,000 farms. Most were used for threshing but as Flora Thompson showed in *Lark Rise to Candleford,* first published in 1939, (which describes her Oxfordshire childhood in the 1890s), they had other uses:

> **Every Autumn appeared a pair of large traction engines, which, posted one on each side of a field, drew a plough across and across by means of a cable. These toured the district under their own steam for hire on the different farms and the outfit included a small caravan . . . for the two drivers to live and sleep in . . . . Such machinery as the farmer owned was horse drawn . . . in harvest time the mechanical reaper was already a familiar sight but . . . men were still mowing with scythes . . . shoulder to begin another.**

A scythe-mower would consider he had done a good day's work if he had cut an acre of grass. A reaping machine (pulled by horses or steam engine) could do ten times as much. Today farmers employ very few workers but use many machines.

Museums of rural life often have photographs and models of nineteenth-century agricultural machinery. Steam traction-engine rallies are quite often held in the summer – consult your local newspaper.

Steam Engines in Industry

In 1863 the *Quarterly Review* remarked that "without doubt the invention of the steam engine is the greatest mechanical triumph which man has yet achieved". By this time, steam power turned the machinery of the "workshop of the world". Even today in many industrial cities you can see the tall factory chimneys of Queen Victoria's reign.

THE VALUE OF THE STEAM ENGINE

Dr Andrew Ure was a strong supporter of industrialization and in his book *Philosophy of Manufactures* (1835) he explained the advantages of the steam engine:

> A manufacturer works a 60 h.p. Boulton & Watt's steam engine, at a power of 120 horses, during the day, and 60 horses during the night . . . therefore a steam horse power is equivalent in working

Joyce's engine, 1851. Try to name the various parts, using the technical terms in the extract from the Illustrated Exhibitor.

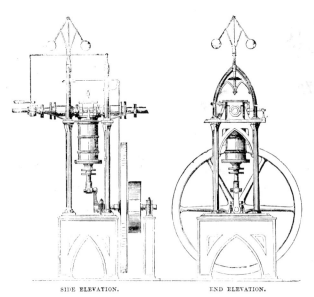

SIDE ELEVATION.   END ELEVATION.

JOYCE'S PENDULOUS STEAM ENGINE

The *Illustrated Exhibitor* described one engine which was used in the textile industry – and also for powering the ice-cream-making machine for the second class refreshment rooms at the Great Exhibition!

> The steam engine of Mr. Joyce of Greenwich is called a 'high-pressure pendulous engine'. The cylinder is suspended by trunnions [pivots] from the top, and the piston gives motion to the crank, on the shafts of which are the fly-wheel and pulley. By a band from

> efficiency to one living horse and one-half the labour of another. But a horse can work at its full efficiency only eight hours out of twenty-four, whereas a steam engine needs no period of repose [rest]; and therefore to make the animal power equal to the physical power, a relay of 1½ fresh horses must be found three times in twenty-four hours, which amounts to 4½ horses daily. Hence a common 60 h.p. does the work of 4½ times 60 horses, or of 270 horses. But the above 60-horse steam engine does one-half more work in 24 hours, or that of 405 horses! The keep [upkeep] of a horse . . .

How do you think Ure carries on with his argument? Try to complete the last sentence in your own words.

In this boiler explosion at a brewery in 1866 two ▷ people were killed and seven injured. Such explosions were frequent. If the pressure in a 30-foot long boiler was released suddenly, several tons of iron would hurtle through the air.

the latter, motion is distributed to various pulleys and shafts, by which a variety of different machines are set and kept in motion. The engine is of simple construction, and does its work well . . . the consumption of fuel is less than 3 lb per h.p. per hour, and there is a saving of one half the space usually occupied by ordinary steam engines.

This was a very efficient engine for its time. However, by the end of the century well-run engines were only using 1½ lb of coal per h.p. per hour. What three advantages are claimed for Joyce's engine?

THE STEAM ENGINE IN MANCHESTER

The author of *The Land We Live In*, written in the middle of the nineteenth century, described the role the steam engine played in one part of the textile industry.

In these power looms steam power may be said to do everything. It unwinds the warp from warpbeam; it lifts and depresses the treddles, by which the warp-threads are placed in the proper position for receiving the weft-threads; it throws the shuttle from side to side, carrying the weft-thread with it; it moves the batten, by which the weft thread is driven up close; and finally, it winds the woven cloth on the cloth-beam which is to receive it. The female who has to manage a pair of looms, has merely to attend to a few minor adjustments . . .

What process is being carried out and which textile is being worked? If you live in northern England or southern Scotland you might be able to visit a mill museum or even a working mill.

Most industries used steam power, and some steam engines remained in use until quite recently. If there is an industrial museum near you (see page 46) find out what sort of steam engines it holds.

Engineers and Public Health

From the mid-nineteenth century onwards thousands of miles of sewage and water pipes and tunnels were built. Thanks to the work of Victorian engineers people in Britain today take clean water and efficient sewage disposal systems for granted. However, although the Victorians built well, 100-year-old brick-lined tunnels and drains are now beginning to crumble. As a result, it is estimated that 30 per cent of the public water supply is being lost. Late twentieth-century engineers are thus faced with rebuilding the system constructed by their Victorian predecessors.

A DANGEROUS SYSTEM OF SEWAGE DISPOSAL

The author of *Old and New London* (c. 1880) described the situation in London before the great public health reforms of the mid-nineteenth century.

> **Previous to the completion of the Main Drainage works . . . on the North side of the Thames there were about 50 main sewers, measuring upwards of 100 miles . . . add to these the private sewers . . . and the mileage of sewage might have been of sufficient length to reach from London to Constantinople. Through these secret channels rolled the refuse of London, in a black murky flood, here and there changing its temperature and colour, as chemical dye-works, sugar-bakers, tallow-melters, and slaughterers added their tributary streams to the pestiferous rolling river. About 31,650,000 gallons of this liquid was poured yearly into the Thames . . .**

What do you think was the result of this system of sewage disposal?

BUILDING A NEW SYSTEM

The Pictorial Handbook of London, published by H.G. Bohn in 1854, described the plans to provide London with an efficient sewage disposal system.

> **On the north side [of the Thames] it is proposed to intercept the whole of the existing sewers before they fall into the river, by means of two intercepting sewers . . . the direction of these intercepting lines is to be made to converge to a point on the eastern bank of the River Lea, where a pumping**

Section of the Holborn Viaduct showing the subways. Note the granite cobbled street, the gas pipes and telegraph pipes, the sewers with links to the street and to houses. What approximate date would you give this picture?

station is to be erected .... From thence the united sewers will flow to a reservoir ... and unless employed for agricultural purposes, the sewage water will there be discharged at such a period of the tide as to prevent its reflux to London ... [and there will be] a total of intercepting sewers of ... 37 miles ... draining an area of 41½ square miles ...

Where is your nearest pumping station? Does it date from the nineteenth century? (Perhaps the architectural style will help you date it.)

SHEFFIELD'S WATER SUPPLY

White's *Sheffield District Directory* of 1868 described how the local water company built two large reservoirs in the 1850s.

An Act [of Parliament] for expanding the water works ... was obtained in 1853. Under the power of this act, the company commenced the formation of those two immense dams, called the Dale Dyke and Agden Reservoirs, in the high moorland valleys of the two chief sources of the River Loxley, near Bradfield, about 8 miles W.N.W. of Sheffield .... The expense of making these reservoirs, and of cutting a tunnel under Stannington Ridge to send water to the town reservoirs ... was estimated at about £100,000.

In 1864 the Bradfield reservoir broke its banks. It contained about 1 million cubic feet of water which flooded the country 12 miles around, causing 250 deaths.

The Cornish engine, used by the East London Waterworks Company to pump water. (The South Kensington Museum is now called the Science Museum.)

THE PROVISION OF WATER

Old and New London described the enormous changes that had taken place in the city's water supply.

In 1833-4, the quantity of water daily supplied by the eight different water companies of London was upwards of 21,000,000 imperial gallons .... In 1876 the average daily supply of the eight companies ... was rather more than 120,000,000 gallons .... The network of pipes underground to convey the water to almost every house in London, must indeed be something surprising ...

Try to find out where the water that you drink comes from.

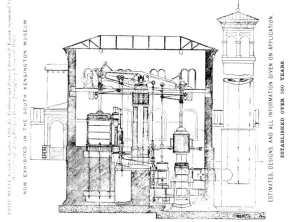

HARVEY & Co., LIMITED, Hayle, Cornwall, and

SINGLE-ACTING CONDENSING ENGINE.

186 & 187, Gresham House, London, E.C.

Engineering and Steel

Before the mid-nineteenth century steel was made by a long and complicated process. Only small amounts were made because production costs were so high. All this was changed by Henry Bessemer. He brought in the age of plentiful and cheap steel. By the end of the century this had expanded man's ability to build and travel.

THE IMPORTANCE OF CARBON

Of all the compounds of iron, none are to be compared with those of carbon in practical importance . . . . When carbon is absent . . . we have wrought iron, which is comparatively soft, malleable, ductile, weldable . . .; when present in certain (small) proportions . . . we have the various kinds of steel, which are highly elastic, malleable, ductile, forgeable, weldable, and capable of receiving very different degrees of hardness by tempering . . . and lastly, when present in greater proportion than in steel, we have cast iron, which is hard, comparatively brittle . . . but not forgeable or weldable. (John Percy, *Metallurgy: The Art of Extracting Metals*

THE BESSEMER PROCESS

To make cheap steel Bessemer planned to blow oxygen into molten cast iron. This would remove the carbon and leave molten steel. In 1855 Bessemer carried out his first experiment with his converter. He described what happened in *An Autobiography* (1905).

About 7 cwt of molten pig [i.e. cast] iron was run into the hopper . . . . All went on quietly for about ten minutes . . . . But soon after, a rapid change took place; in fact the silicon had been quietly consumed and the oxygen next uniting with the carbon sent up an ever-increasing stream of sparks and a

from their Ores and Adapting Them to Various Purposes of Manufacture, 1864)

You can see from this extract that steel has all the advantages of wrought and cast iron but none of their disadvantages.

Two views of the Bessemer Converter, looking like a very large cement mixer. It is fixed on a pivot which enables the vessel to be tipped, thus allowing the molten steel to be run off.

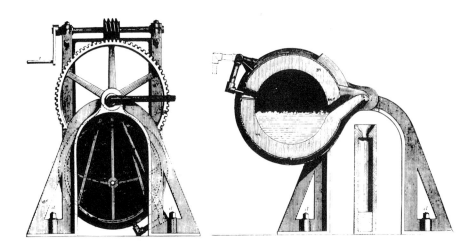

voluminous white flame. Then followed a succession of mild explosions, throwing molten slags and splashes of metal high into the air, the apparatus becoming a veritable volcano in a state of active eruption . . . in ten minutes more the eruption had ceased, the flame died down, and the process was completed. On tapping the converter into a shallow pan . . . and forming the metal into an ingot, it was found to be wholly decarbonised malleable iron . . .

Find out how the work of Siemens and the Gilchrist Thomas cousins further improved steel production.

STEEL RAILS

In 1862 the *Illustrated Guide to Sheffield and Neighbourhood* by J. Brailsford and H. Pawson noted:

The vast superiority of steel, on account of its great durability, cannot be disputed. For instance, at the Pimlico station [in London] on some parts of the London and North Western, and on the Caledonian Railway, steel rails have been put down, and have been found at the end of the year to be nearly as good as new, whereas the old iron rails required to be renewed about once in three months.

Steel did not finally triumph over iron until after 1879. In that year the Tay Bridge (see page 38) collapsed. It had been built of wrought and cast iron.

This advertisement dates from 1862. Compare the uses to which steel was put at this time to the 1889 list of uses. (Crinoline steel was fine strips of steel made up to form the framework for women's dresses.)

THE AGE OF STEEL

In 1889 the *Quarterly Review* listed the uses to which steel had been successfully applied.

(1) Ships and Armour [i.e. armour plate for warships]
(2) Guns [i.e. naval guns and artillery]
(3) Railway work [i.e. rails and locomotives]
(4) Miscellaneous uses [i.e. boilers, water pipes, beams used in buildings].

In 1876 the make of Bessemer steel in the U.K. was 400,000 tons . . . . In 1884 the total production of Bessemer steel ingots in the Kingdom was 1,300,000; in 1887 it had risen to 2,000,000 tons, an increase of 59 per cent in three years. Of this amount no less than 1,000,000 tons were used for rails . . .

The facts and figures embodied in this article are our justification for calling the present period emphatically the Age of Steel.

Make a list of all the qualities that steel possesses which make it so suitable for a wide variety of uses.

W. H. BROWN AND CO.,

TRADE W.H.B. MARK.

ALBION IRON AND STEEL WORKS,
SHEFFIELD,

MANUFACTURERS OF

INDIAN, SPANISH, AND SWEDISH

BAR IRON AND STEEL:

Cast Steel, for Wire, in Rods or Coils; for Needles, Hackle Pins, Umbrella Ribs, Fish Hooks, Spiral Springs, Telegraphs, Pit Ropes, Marine Cables, and other purposes;

CAST STEEL IN RODS,

For Spindles, Razors, Scissors, Table, Pen & Pocket Knives, Hammers, Chisels, Edge Tools, and Bars for Railway Carriage and Locomotive Engine Springs, &c., &c.

ALSO, MANUFACTURERS OF

CRINOLINE STEEL,

In Sheets, flattened Wire, or cut into Strips, Hardened, and Tempered, ready for the covering process, and any other purpose to which Steel may be applied.

"Might Have Beens"

We sometimes read in the newspaper or hear on the television of engineering projects being cancelled. Plans for a new aircraft are shelved or trains which tilt on bends are found to tilt too much. Victorian engineers at times were also disappointed when their plans were cancelled or found to be impracticable.

THE ATMOSPHERIC RAILWAY

The idea of finding some alternative to the steam locomotive attracted many engineers. In 1844 Daniel Gooch went with Isambard Kingdom Brunel to Ireland to see an atmospheric railway. As he recorded in his diary, he was not impressed:

> The gradient and curves were both very bad. Mr. Brunel was at this time constructing the South Devon, and as the gradients and curves of that line were also very bad it was proposed to use the atmospheric system on it . . . . From the calculations I then made of the power used to work the engines I found I could do the work much cheaper with locomotives. The result of our visit, however, was the determination to use the atmospheric pipes on the South Devon. I could not then understand how Mr. Brunel could be so misled as he was . . . . [But] he had

THOMSON'S ROAD STEAMERS

A rather odd solution to the problem of public transport in the quickly growing Victorian cities emerged in the late 1860s. *The Graphic*, an illustrated news magazine, gave some details on 11 June 1870.

> The great peculiarity in this road steamer is that the wheels are bound round to the depth of 5 inches with an India-rubber tire . . . . The steamer is commonly used to draw an omnibus or carriage . . . . On May 25 [1870] an experiment was made in Edinburgh

> so much faith in his being able to improve it that he shut his eyes to the consequences of failure . . . . The line was laid with all the care possible . . . . and it miserably failed . . .

This episode damaged Brunel's reputation. See if you can find out more about how the atmospheric railway was supposed to work, and why it did not work in practice.

The road steamer. Note the similarities and differences between this omnibus and the buses of today. Does this road steamer look like a practical proposition to you?

with the steamer and omnibus. The omnibus has only two wheels . . . it is built to carry 65 passengers . . . the journey, which was to Leith and back, was accomplished without the slightest hitch, and the whole of the party expressed themselves highly satisfied at the performance of Mr. Thomson's ingenious and useful invention.

Why do you think the engine had rubber tyres? Neither Thomson's invention, nor any sort of steam road carriage, was ever widely used – think of reasons why this was.

THE CHANNEL TUNNEL

Today there are plans to build a tunnel across the English Channel. This is not a new idea. In 1881 tunnelling actually began. On 3 July 1882 *The Times* described the progress that had been made.

M. de Lesseps and a party of French engineers . . . were lowered six at a time in an iron 'skip' down the shaft into the tunnel. At the bottom of this shaft, 163 feet below the surface of the ground, the mouth of the tunnel was reached . . . so evenly had the boring machine done its work that we seemed to be looking along a great tube . . . and as the glowing electric lamps . . . showed fainter and fainter in the far distance, the tunnel, for anything one could tell from appearances, might have had its outlet in France.

In fact, the tunnel at this time was 1900 yards long and about 150 feet below the sea. Notice the use of a tunnelling machine (invented by Colonel Frederick Beaumont) and of electric light. With what great engineering work do we link de Lessep's name?

SIR GARNET WOLSELEY

Work on the Channel tunnel stopped in 1882 after the Government, giving way to public opinion, forbade any further work. One of the leading anti-tunnel spokesmen was the popular military hero, Wolseley, who warned:

A couple of thousand armed men might easily come through the tunnel in a train at night, avoiding all suspicion by being dressed as ordinary passengers, and the first thing we would know about it would be by finding the fort at our end of the tunnel . . . in the hands of an enemy . . . and then England would be at the mercy of the invader. (Quoted in P. Beaver, *A History of Tunnels*, 1972)

Remember that in the nineteenth century Britain relied on the Royal Navy for her defence and that many people regarded France as our most likely enemy.

An 1881 map showing the route of the proposed Channel Tunnel. Watch carefully in the newspapers for stories on the current plans for building a tunnel under the Channel. You might be able to build up a scrap-book of newspaper articles.

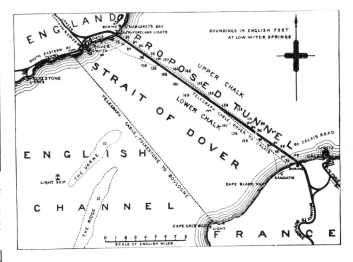

Disaster and Triumph

The later years of Victoria's reign saw the building of two great railway bridges in Scotland. One crossed the Firth of Tay. It collapsed a year after it was opened. The other bridge was built across the Firth of Forth; it still stands today.

THE TAY BRIDGE DISASTER

The late nineteenth-century Scottish "poet" William McGonnagall described the tragedy in verse (*Poetic Gems* 1890)

> Beautiful Railway Bridge of the Silv'ry Tay!
> Alas! I am very sorry to say
> That 90 lives have been taken away
> On the last Sabbath day of 1879
> Which will be remembered for a very long time
> . . . .
> So the train mov'd slowly along the Bridge of Tay
> Until it was about midway,
> Then the central girders with a crash gave way,
> And down went the train and passengers into the Tay!
> . . . .

A PUBLIC INQUIRY

The engineer responsible for the Tay Bridge was Thomas Bouch. The bridge was opened, with much ceremony, on 31 May 1878 but, on 28 December 1879, during a violent hurricane, the central portion collapsed. The Court of Inquiry set up to investigate the disaster presented its report to Parliament in June 1880.

> The conclusion then, to which we have come, is that this bridge was badly designed, badly constucted and badly

> I must now conclude my lay
> By telling the world fearlessly without the least dismay,
> That your central girders would not have given way,
> At least many sensible men do say,
> Had they been supported on each side with buttresses
> . . . .

McGonagall was not a very good poet, but he did reflect the anger of the public at the news of the disaster.

The first and second Tay Bridges.

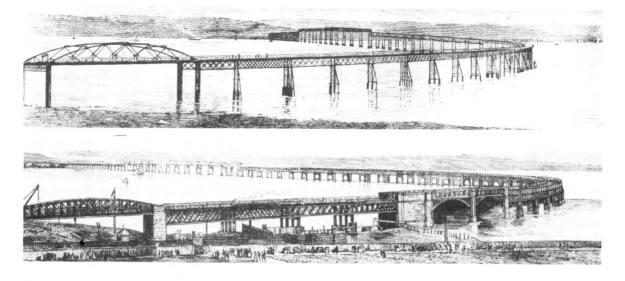

maintained, and that its downfall was due to inherent defects in the structure which sooner or later mast have brought it down. Sir Thomas Bouch is, in our opinion, mainly to blame.

Bouch died in 1880 – his health had collapsed under the strain.

Do you think the case of Thomas Bouch bears out those criticisms made by Matthew Arnold (on page 7) on the training of engineers? Work on rebuilding the Tay bridge began in 1882 and was completed in 1887.

THE FORTH BRIDGE

In July 1888 the *Illustrated London News* described the building of the 1½-mile long bridge. It was now possible to travel by train, without interruption, from London to Aberdeen and beyond.

The construction of the great railway bridge to cross the Firth of Forth at Queensferry . . . where the opposite shores of Fifeshire and Linlithgowshire nearly approach each other, with the rocky islet of Inchgarrie between them,

is one of the grandest works of modern engineering. It was designed, for the North British Railway Company, by Sir John Fowler and Mr. Benjamin Baker, and has been four or five years in actual progress.

The water in the middle of the Firth of Forth is 200 feet deep and so:

It was impossible to erect piers anywhere but on this islet; hence the bridge must rest on three main piers, one at South Queensferry, one at Inchgarrie, and one on the Fife shore, besides two supplementary piers . . . each opening of the Forth Bridge is ⅓ of a mile in clear span; which unprecedented width is spanned by a steel structure made up of two cantilevers or brackets, projecting 675 feet from the piers . . . . The cantilevers project about 400 feet from the piers.

What two reasons are given for the siting of the bridge? Where is meant by the expression "North British"?

"A bridge, in addition to doing duty in the engineering sense, should convey a feeling of satisfaction to all who behold it, simply as a study of art, giving gratification from its fitness and beauty . . ." (The Engineer, 11 May 1886). Do you feel that the Forth Bridge lives up to this standard?
The frontispiece to this book shows one of the central sections of the Forth Bridge under construction.

In the mid-nineteenth century, London's roads were clogged with horse-drawn vehicles. One solution was to construct railways underground. By the end of the century London had an extensive underground system part of which ran beneath the embankments along the River Thames.

THE FIRST UNDERGROUND RAILWAY

The world's first underground railway was opened in 1863. The Metropolitan Railway extended 4½ miles from Paddington to Finsbury (it is now part of the Circle Line). *Cassell's Illustrated History* written a few years later, was full of admiration.

> **It had to be carried underneath the streets of the busiest of cities, down where the soil was honeycombed with other works – gas pipes, water-mains, drains and sewers. It had to undermine without damaging the foundations of houses and churches, and other public and private buildings. The cost was fabulous, being upwards of £150,000 per mile.**

The main reason why the first underground railway was so expensive was that the greater part of it was constructed just below street level on the "cut and cover" principle. Later undergrounds were built much deeper to avoid disturbing drains, sewers and foundations of buildings.

A SMOKELESS TRAIN

One difficulty facing the engineers of the Metropolitan Railway was that of using steam locomotives underground.

> **This Mr. Fowler surmounted by inventing an engine which, in the open air, works like a common locomotive,**

A DISAGREEMENT

In his memoirs Daniel Gooch was scathing about Fowler's engine.

> **1862 . . . Mr. Fowler had, with the assistance of Messrs Stephenson and Co. of Newcastle, designed and built an engine for this purpose [i.e. working underground] of the most extraordinary description and, as a**

The picture illustrates the principle of "cut and cover" and the problems associated with steam locomotives in the "Underground".

> **but when in the tunnel, consumes its own smoke, or rather makes no smoke, and by condensing its own steam, gives off not a particle of vapour.** (John Timbs, *Wonderful Inventions,* 1867)

The fireless engine designed by the Metropolitan engineer, John Fowler, used hot bricks to maintain steam.

Thames Embankment

trial soon found, quite useless. I simply made an ordinary engine but fitted it with tanks under the boiler into which I discharged the waste steam . . . . This engine I found answered very well and has been the one used.

With construction of deep-level underground railways, a new type of motive power was needed. What was used from 1890 onwards?

THE EMBANKMENT OF THE THAMES

For thirty years engineers had argued for making wide embankments along the north side of the Thames from Westminster to Blackfriars. The two main reasons in favour were to control the river and to provide a thoroughfare between the Houses of Parliament and the City of London. In 1860 plans were made to build a trunk sewer parallel to the river and the embankment project became a reality. Fowler took advantage of the scheme to extend the underground. The first section of the embankment was completed in 1869.

The total area of land reclaimed from the river amounts to 37½ acres . . . . Within the Embankment wall . . . is placed the low-level Intercepting Sewer . . . above it is a subway for gas

and water pipes . . . . The Metropolitan District Railway enters the land reclaimed by the Embankment between Cannon Row and Westminster Bridge . . . the level of the rails is generally 17½ feet below the surface of the road, which is carried over the railway by cast-iron girders and brick arches, the upper surface of the arches being 18 inches below the surface of the road. (*Old and New London, c.* 1880)

Study the section of the Thames Embankment carefully and relate it to the description above. Note the large railway terminus building above ground (Blackfriars Station) and the steam locomotive in the tunnel.

If there are any rivers running through your town see if they have been embanked and when it was done. (Look out for a stone commemorating the official opening of the embankment.)

Section of the Thames Embankment, 1867. Note the water pipes (1), the low-level sewer (2), the train (3) and the pneumatic railway (4) built to transmit letters, newspapers and parcels by tubes laid under the street.

Contractors and Navvies

No book on Victorian engineering would be complete without some reference to the contractors and navvies who actually carried out the work. Without their efforts the ideas of the engineers would have remained just that.

RAILWAY CONTRACTORS

F.S. Williams in his book *Our Iron Roads* (1852) explained why railway companies used contractors rather than organizing the construction of the line themselves.

> The execution of the works is seldom left in the hands of the actual proprietors. Railway Directors are usually connected with 'city' life [i.e. they knew how to raise the money to build the railway] . . . and hence it is found best to give the formation of the line to contractors who engage to complete the various parts at a specified cost. Contracting for railway-making has thus become a great business; and some experienced and wealthy men will now undertake the completion of the entire works of a long line . . . . The chief contractors . . . sub-let the different works to sub-contractors, giving the earthworks to one, the masonry to another, and the ballasting to a third . . .

What would have influenced a company when choosing a contractor?

"Taylor Woodrow" and "Mowlem" are two large contracting firms of today. Look out for their signs on motorway bridges and on large buildings.

THOMAS BRASSEY AT WORK

One of the greatest of Victorian contractors was Thomas Brassey. In *The Life and Labours of Mr. Brassey* (1872) the author, Sir Arthur Helps, described the great contractor's way of working.

> When Mr. Brassey took out a contract, he let out portions of the work to sub-contractors . . . . I find that the sub-contracts varied from £5,000 to £25,000; and that the number of men employed upon them would be from one to three hundred . . . . If he came down to look at a line of railway, he would . . . regard easy works as beneath his notice: he never looked at them; but if there was a difficult point . . . then there was something to look at . . . . He economized his time and brought his experience and judgement to bear where they were useful . . . and as he went along . . . in these inspections he remembered even the navvies, and saluted them by their names.

List the personal qualities you think Brassey had. Why did he use sub-contractors?

A REMARKABLE CLASS

> The 'railway navvies' . . . were men drawn by the attraction of good wages from all parts of the Kingdom; and they were ready for any sort of hard work . . . . Their expertness in all sorts of earthwork, in embanking boring and well-sinking – their practical knowledge of the nature of soils and rocks . . . were very very great; and, rough-looking though they were, many of them were as important in their own

Many navvies died in the construction of Britain's railways, bridges and tunnels. This memorial, which is in the shape of a tunnel and is in the churchyard at Otley in Yorkshire, commemorates the navvies killed in building the Bramhope Tunnel on the Leeds and Thirsk Railway, 1845-9.

THE LIFE OF A "NAVVY"

This man was interviewed by Henry Mayhew, the famous social investigator, in 1849.

I have been a navvy for about eighteen years. The first work that I done was on the Manchester and Liverpool. I was a lad then. I used to grease the wagons .... The next place I had after that was the London and Brummagen [Birmingham]. There I went as a horse driver .... I went to work on the London to York .... I stopped on this line ... until last spring. Then all the work on it stopped, and I dare say 2,000 men were thrown out of employ on one day .... I went away from there over to the Brummagen and Beechly branch line ... then I came to Copenhagen-fields on the London and York – the London end, Sir ...

department as the contractor or the engineer.

During the railway-making period the navvy wandered about from one public work to another .... They displayed great pluck, and seemed to disregard danger. (S. Smiles, *Lives of the Engineers*, 1862)

Find out the origin of the word "navvy". In what ways do you think the work of the twentieth-century "navvy" is easier, and safer, than that of his Victorian predecessor?

A DANGEROUS JOB

The author of this article, published in a magazine in 1861-2, left his rural home in the 1840s to work as a navvy.

Once, when I was in Dorsetshire, I was in a tunnel that fell in at both ends. There was only one man and me and some horses buried in it, and he drove a hole through the ground (he was about 8 hours doing it), and then he and me got out, and left the horses in for 3 days and nights. We had to lower corn and water to them through the hole, till we could dig them out; but we were none of us hurt. (Quoted in J. Burnett, *Useful Toil*, 1974)

abutment	a pier or wall which supports something.
aggregate	total.
anvil	a heavy block of iron on which heated metal is hammered into shape.
boring	the process of digging a tunnel, especially when using a revolving tool.
brazier	a metal container for burning coals.
Caledonia	the Roman name for Scotland.
cantilever	projecting beam.
carbon	a black chemical found in charcoal and coal.
cast iron	iron shaped by being poured when molten into a mould.
coffer-dam	a water-tight enclosure from which the water is pumped to obtain a dry foundation for bridges, piers etc.
combustible	capable of burning.
compound	something made up of several parts or ingredients.
condensing	the process of turning steam into water.
crank	a bent rod used to turn an engine or machine.
crucible	a container in which metals are fused together.
cut and cover	a method of building a tunnel by excavating a large trench and then covering with a brick roof.
cylinder	a solid or hollow tube, part of an engine in which a piston moves.
defective	faulty.
deficient	lacking.
draughtsman	someone who draws plans of buildings, machines etc.
ductile	capable of being drawn into wire.
dyke	a long ridge of earth.
elastic	something which can stretch and go back to its original size afterwards.
eminence	rising ground.
file	a metal tool with a rough surface used for making things smooth.
forge	shape metal by heating in a fire and hammering.
foundry	a place where metal is melted and moulded.
freight	goods, cargo.
gazetteer	a geographical dictionary.
gin	a primitive engine in which a vertical shaft is turned by horses driving a horizontal beam or yoke in a circle.
girder	a long, thick bar of iron or steel.
gorse-bruiser	a machine for crushing gorse.
hydraulic	worked by water or other liquid.
ingot	a lump of metal.
lattice	a structure of wood or bars crossing each other.
malleable	metals that can be shaped by hammering.
micrometer	an instrument for measuring minute differences of dimension.
millwright	a word used in the eighteenth and early nineteenth centuries for a mechanical engineer.
molten	melted, usually by great heat.
oscillating	swinging to and fro.
permanent way	the finished road-bed of a railway.
pier	a piece of solid upright masonry supporting the superstructue of a bridge.
pig iron	cast iron in the shape of an oblong block.
piles	pieces of timber driven into the ground, usually under water, as the foundation of a building.
piston	the part of an engine which moves inside the cylinder.
pulley	a wheel with a groove in the rim for a rope to run over, used for lifting things.
riveting	the fastening together of metal plates.
scythe	a tool with a long curved blade for cutting grass or corn.

shoring	the propping up of a trench or wall.
shuttle	part of a loom or some other machine that moves to and fro.
skip	cage or bucket in which men or materials are raised and lowered in mines.
slag	the waste product of an iron or coal works.
superstructure	what rests on top of a foundation.
superintendent	a supervisor.
telegraph	the instantaneous carrying of messages to any distance by means of two instruments connected by electricity.
tempering	the process by which steel is brought to the required degree of hardness.
tender	wheeled vehicle carrying coal attached to a locomotive.
threshing	the process by which grain is separated from the straw.
valve	a device for controlling the flow of liquid or gas.
viaduct	a long bridge with many arches carrying a road or railway.

Money

Always look at what money and wages could buy rather than at what seem low prices to us. It is no use butter being 4p a pound if we only earn 50p a week. Remember that there were 12 old pence (d.) in a shilling (s.) and 20 shillings to the pound. 6d. was the equivalent of 2½p, a shilling (1/-) 5p.

Weights and Measures

1 foot (30.48 cm); 1 mile (1.61 km); 1 hundredweight (cwt) (50.802 kg); 1 ton (1.016 tonne); 1 gallon (4.544 litres); 1 acre (0.4047 hectares).

□□□□□□□□□□□□□□□ Date List □□□□□□□□□□□□□□□□

1836 Construction of Great Western Railway started.
1838 Race across Atlantic by *Sirius* and *Great Western*. "Tug of war" between *Rattler* and *Alecto*.
1839 James Nasmyth invented the steam hammer.
1840 Joseph Whitworth produced first standard range of screws.
1843 *Great Britain* launched. Marc Brunel's Thames tunnel for foot passengers opened.
1848 James Usher patented a steam plough.
1850 Newcastle High Level Bridge and Britannia Bridge opened.
1851 Royal Border Bridge across River Tweed at Berwick opened. Great Exhibition ("of Arts and Manufactures") held in London.
1855 Joseph Whitworth produced very accurate micrometer. Henry Bessemer revealed his revolutionary method of steel production.
1857 *Great Eastern* launched.
1859 Royal Albert Bridge opened.
1861 Siemen brothers patent the "open-hearth" method of steel production.
1863 The world's first underground railway opened in London.
1864 Clifton Suspension Bridge opened.

1865 Red Flag Act restricted speed of mechanically propelled road vehicles to 4 m.p.h. (repealed 1896).
1866 *Great Eastern* laid first trans-Atlantic telegraph cable.
1875 Sidney Gilchrist Thomas and his cousin Percy Gilchrist discovered the "basic process" of steel production.
1878 Severn Bridge opened. Tay Bridge disaster.
1880 Albert Dock in London opened.
1884 Charles Parsons invented the steam turbine.
1886 Severn Railway Tunnel opened.
1887 Second Tay Bridge completed.
1889 S.Z. de Ferranti's Deptford electical power station opened.
1890 Forth Railway Bridge opened.
1892 Final end of the broad gauge on the Great Western Railway. Completion of first masonry dam at Vyrnwy in Wales.
1893 Manchester Ship Canal opened.
1895 Frederick Lanchester built first British four wheeled car. Charles Parsons built the world's first turbine-powered vessel, *Turbinia*.
1901 The first large turbine-powered steamer launched, appropriately called *King Edward*.

This list is only a personal selection from the many museums there are in the United Kingdom which deal with aspects of Victorian engineering. There is a very useful booklet published each year called *Museums and Galleries in Great Britain and Ireland*, which not only gives you a list of all the museums in the British Isles, but also gives the cost of admission and times of opening. Also very useful for those who wish to explore the work of Brunel and Stephenson are the gazetteers in D. Beckett's two books. These list all the major engineering achievements of, and sites connected with, the two men, together with instructions on how best to get to them, either by road or rail.

Armley Mills, Leeds (models of steam powered Victorian agricultural machinery and also stationary steam engines).

Barrow-in-Furness Museum, Cumbria (collection of model ships).

Bristol Industrial Museum (useful for steam powered transport).

British Engineering, Hove, East Sussex (a large collection of exhibits covering engineering history housed in a Victorian Water Pumping Station).

Brunel Atmospheric Railway, Starcross, Near Exeter (one of the pumping houses, dating from 1845, which now houses an exhibition and a working atmospheric railway).

Camden Works, Museum of Bath at Work (the entire stock-in-trade of a Victorian brass founder general engineer).

Chalk Pits Museum, near Arundel, West Sussex (engine house and stationary steam engines).

Clydebank District Museum, Dunbarton (exhibits relating to ship-building).

Coldharbour Mill, Cullompton, Devon, (application of steam power to the textile industry).

Cornish Engines, Camborne, Cornwall, (two great beam engines of the nineteenth century).

Darlington Railway Museum (early railway history)

Exeter Maritime Museum (contains Brunel's 1844 drag-boat for clearing mud from Bridgwater Dock. It is the world's oldest working steamboat).

Great Western Railway Museum, Swindon (historic G.W.R. locomotives and many other exhibits).

Holkham Hall, near Wells-next-the-Sea, Norfolk (Victorian agricultural machinery).

Hunday National Tractor and Farm Museum, Stocksfield, Northumberland (many stationary engines and Victorian reaping and threshing machinery.)

Industrial Museum, Nottingham (especially for the mid-nineteenth-century beam engine).

Industrial Museum, Sheffield (very useful for iron and steel engineering, plus an impressive working steam engine).

Ironbridge Gorge Museum, Telford, Shropshire (particularly the Blists Hill Open Air Museum).

Kew Bridge Engines Trust and Water Supply Museum, London (a large collection of water-pumping steam engines and the world's largest working beam engine).

Leicestershire Museum of Technology, Leicester (especially an impressive beam engine).

Monkwearmouth Station Museum, Sunderland (railway rolling stock).

Museum of Science and Engineering, Newcastle upon Tyne (ship-building).

Museum of Science and Industry, Birmingham (steam engines and machine tools).

Museum of Transport, Glasgow (land transport and ship models).

National Maritime Museum, London (essential for the history of marine engineering).

National Mining Museum, Retford, Nottinghamshire (coal mine engineering).

National Railway Museum, York (marvellous for all those interested in railway engineering).

National Tramway Museum, Crick, near Matlock, Derbyshire.

North of England Open Air Museum, Beamish, Co. Durham (tram and locomotive rides).

North Western . Museum of Science and Industry, Manchester (many working machines).

Science Museum, London (essential for those interested in all aspects of engineering).

SS Great Britain, Bristol.

Welsh Industrial and Maritime Museum, Cardiff (machinery and motive power).

Book List

This is a list of some books that I have found useful in writing *Victorian Engineering:*

Andrews, A., *Wonders of Victorian Engineering* (1978)

Beaver, P., *A History of Tunnels*, Peter Davies (1972)

Beckett, D., *Brunel's Britain* (1980) and *Stephenson's Britain* (1984), David & Charles

Brownlee, W., *Warrior. – The First Modern Battleship*, Cambridge University Press (1985)

Brunel, I., *The Life of Isambard Kingdom Brunel* (1870); reprinted David & Charles (1971)

Buchanan, R.A., *Industrial Archaeology in Britain*, Penguin (1972)

Burstall, A.F., *A History of Mechanical Engineering*, Faber (1963)

Coleman, T., *The Railway Navvies* (1965)

Cossons, N., *The B.P. Book of Industrial Archaeology* (1975)

Cunningham, C., *Building for the Victorians* Cambridge University Press (1985)

Guest, G.M., *A Brief History of Engineering*, Harrap (1974)

Hadfield, C., *Atmospheric Railways*, David & Charles (1967)

Hay, P., *Brunel: Engineering Giant*, B.T. Batsford (1985)

Holt E. and Perham, M., *Historic Transport* (1979) and *Industrial Archaeology* (1980), Evans

Lambert, A.J., *Nineteenth-Century Railway History Through the Illustrated London News*, David & Charles (1984)

Pugsley, A. (ed.), *The Works of Isambard Kingdom Brunel*, Cambridge University Press (1976)

Prebble, J., *The High Girders (The Tay Bridge Disaster)*, Secker & Warburg (1956)

Richards, J.M., *The National Trust Book of Bridges*, Jonathan Cape (1984)

Rolt, L.T.C., *George and Robert Stephenson*, Penguin (1960); *Great Engineers*, Bell (1962); *Isambard Kingdom Brunel*, Penguin (1957), and *Victorian Engineering*, Penguin (1970)

Semler E.G. (ed.), *Engineering Heritage*, (2 Vols) (1966)

Smiles, S., *Industrial Biography* (1863) and *Lives of the Engineers Vol. III* (1862)

Thompson, H., *Engineers and Engineering* (1976)

Index